How to Get a Job After Law School

(The Job Won't Find You)

Miller Leonard

Table of Contents

1) **Introduction** 1
2) **Decide Where You Want to Live** 4
3) **What Type of Law Do You Think You Want to Practice?** 8
   - A. Clinics 8
   - B. Career Services 9
   - C. What Things Do You Like to Do? 10
   - D. Practice Series Books 11
   - E. Continuing Legal Education Seminars 12
   - F. My Story 12
   - G. What do You Want? 13
4) **Networking** 14
   - A. You're Part of a Profession 15
   - B. Get Used to Asking for Help 15
   - C. Some People Will Say "No" 15
   - D. Get a Plan – Any Plan is Better Than No Plan .. 16
   - E. Find a Mentor 16
   - Final Thoughts 17
5) **Small Markets** 18
6) **The Hidden Job Market and Your 5 Year Plan** ... 21

	5 years	22
7)	**Adjuncts**	25
8)	**LinkedIn**	28
9)	**Why You Need to Start Following the Legal Job Market**	30
10)	**Closing Thoughts**	32
11)	**Appendix 1**	34
12)	**Appendix 2**	37

Introduction

Most of us go to law school in order to get a job as a lawyer. Yet only 10% of all law students will get a job through On Campus Interviews. This figure, even if it is off by a few percentage points, is stunning.

So how do you get a job as a lawyer if you don't secure one through OCI's? This is the purpose of this book: To help you get a job as a lawyer.

But before we get into the book and the suggestions, I want to take you back in time. If you will, take a journey with me.

On a sunny day, in mid-May, I walked into my law school for the last time to get items out of the law school office the school provided to 3L's. As I walked into school, two classmates asked me where I was going to work. I had no answer. Even though I had secured two internships and worked at two different law firms during law school, I had no job lined up and I had no prospects. I was, in a word, lost.

25 years later, I can see all of the mistakes I made. I don't want you to make the same mistakes. And I want to give you hope that you can and will get a job as a lawyer. That is why I am writing this book.

Before you start reading, remember a few things:

- Feel free to throw out any suggestion.
- There is no right plan.
- Getting started is better than not starting at all.
- The process is not a sprint, it is a marathon.
- Learn to enjoy the journey.
- So much of your success as a practicing lawyer has nothing to do with how well you do in law school or the law school you attend. Rather, it has to do with your network.

The end goal of this book is to help you develop a networking plan. The plan will be yours. And the plan will enable you to take the steps to get a job, make friends, gain colleagues, and learn more about the practice of the law.

Does this book guarantee success? No. Nobody can guarantee success and no plan is 100% accurate. That said, I have seen the tips in this book work time and time again. Why? Because most legal jobs are hidden and most legal jobs are the product of the network you develop.

A word of encouragement: You can build a network. It doesn't matter if you aren't the most out-going person. It doesn't matter if you know nobody in the legal field. It doesn't matter if you are a first-generation lawyer. It doesn't matter if you are in the bottom of your class. It doesn't matter if you are attending a T14 school or a school in the bottom tier.

As you read this book, I encourage you to do the following:

- Be open to the suggestions given.
- Commit to creating your own networking plan.

- Commit to spending consistent time implementing your networking plan.
- Remember that everyone who is competing for a job as a lawyer is a lawyer.

This book isn't very long. We are conditioned in law school to write lengthy tomes. Then you start practicing and nobody wants you to write like you did during your collegiate and law school days. This book is written by a practicing lawyer in a style geared towards the practice of law. My goal is to get you a job. It's to get you to use the tips I am suggesting.

The jobs exist. The map to getting the jobs doesn't. This is a map to the job you want.

1) Decide Where You Want to Live

The practice of law is, despite the changes in technology and the changes to how we practice, largely centered upon the geographic area where a law firm is located. This is even more true the smaller the firm or if you work for a government agency.

Since law schools are scattered across the country, many people go to a law school in an area where they do not intend to live. But even if you do attend a law school in the area you want to live, the suggestions of this book are applicable – you just don't have to figure out where you want to live so you can skip ahead.

Deciding where you want to live is important for your networking plan. So take some time to determine where you want to live in order to focus your networking plan and get the most out of it.

Having moved my practice after 10 years in one city and state, I can attest to the challenges of finding a legal job outside of the area one goes to law school. But it isn't impossible and the sooner you figure out where you want to live, the quicker you can start making connections.

Narrowing down where you want to live can be a challenge. In order to help you in this process, I have developed some questions that I ask law students who I work with.

Take some time and put thought into the following questions:

- Where is your family located?
- Do you want to be located away from family? If you do, how far away do you want to be?
- How important is it to fit in with the "values" of the area you live? This isn't an endorsement of any particular value or belief, rather it is about you and what you value and believe.
- Do you describe yourself as conservative, liberal, or does it matter? Do you know the politics of the area you want to live?
- What is the cost of living in the area you want to live?
- Does the area you want to live embrace the things you enjoy doing? For instance, if you like to hike and enjoy open spaces, are such things available? Or, if church is important to you, is there a church you like and where you can thrive?
- If you have children or plan on having children, how are the schools? This is very important. Don't assume the schools are good just because an area is "nice."
- If you are married or have a significant other, are they open to moving? If they are open to moving, is it also a place that they like and want to live? Can they find work?
- Why do you want to move to the area?
- Have you been to the area you want to move outside of a vacation?

- Is the area you want to move to growing economically?
- If you like to travel, is the area you want to move to someplace with a good airport or close to the areas you like to visit?

There are, of course, a myriad of other questions you can ask yourself about the place you want to live. Living in Colorado, a place where many people want to move, I often speak with law students who are going to school outside of Colorado but who want to move to the state. These questions, and one's like them, are the questions we go over. The purpose is to try to hone down the area or areas the student is interested in so that we can then build a networking plan.

Taking a more in depth look at these questions is vital. Moving is hard. It's expensive. So you want to put the necessary time into finding out about the areas you have interest in before you take the leap. For instance, before I moved to Colorado, my wife and I visited a number of times and looked at various areas. We also went to the other area we thought we might like and looked at both places with an eye towards daily life rather than vacation life.

Two things stand out to me about moving. First, you want to move to a place where you feel at home. Having community is important. Second, you want to move to a place that isn't economically decaying. That doesn't necessarily mean a big city. Many smaller communities are thriving. Living in an economically thriving area will help your career opportunities.

The other aspect of moving is family. If you are a traditional law student, you are graduating around the age of 25. You likely aren't thinking too much about taking care of elderly parents. And if you don't have kids, you may not be thinking about having your kids around your parents yet. I encourage you to think about these two issues. I don't have the answer to what is right for you but it is worth thinking 10 – 15 years down the road if you are moving to a new area.

Next, as you think about where you want to live, it is important to also have an idea as to what type of law you want to practice. For instance, if your dream job is being a United States Attorney, you will want to make sure that such a job exists in the town you want to live in – and this goes for any practice area.

After you have gone through the questions outlined, look into the amount of money the area you are interested invests in its court system. Some states do a good job investing in their court system. Others don't and have attacked the funding of the courts for years. This isn't, necessarily, a reason not to move to a state, but you should understand how the state you are wanting to move to values and funds its court system.

Moving is not easy. But the adventure of moving is indescribable. Moving allows you, in many ways, to recreate yourself and chart your own course. If you want to move away from either the area you are going to school or the area you grew up, embrace the challenge. You'll find that the spirit of the journey will aid and assist you as you build your network. After all, if you are a stranger, you have to force yourself to go out and meet people.

2) What Type of Law Do You Think You Want to Practice?

Deciding what type of law you want to practice is, for many, difficult. If you are a first generation law student, like I was, you may find it even harder since you may only know of a few areas of practice. Deciding what area or areas you are interested in practicing is essential to focus your networking.

A. Clinics

Outside of clinics, law school doesn't help you figure out what type of law you want to practice, at least it didn't help me. This is especially true of the required classes that you take as these classes, by and large, focus on the law related to the subject and rarely deal with the practice side of that area of law.

The easiest way to gain exposure to a practice area is to do a clinic. Many law schools have clinics and some have more than one. This is a fantastic resource and one that you must take advantage of if you are able. For instance, if you want to be a Public Defender and your law school offers a Criminal Defense Clinic, you need to do the clinic.

Thankfully, law schools have expanded their clinical opportunities. I cannot emphasize enough how crucial it is to do a clinic. Sometimes I will talk with a law student and they will tell me that they really don't have an interest in any of the clinics offered at their school. My advice is to find the one that most interests you and to do that one.

B. Career Services

Career Services gets maligned. There are two reasons for this: 1) Career Services didn't used to offer much more than OCI help; 2) Unrealistic expectations.

Let's tackle the unrealistic expectations since most Career Service offices offer much more assistance than they did in the past. If you are expecting Career Services to find you a job, this isn't a strategy that will bear fruit. Rather, view Career Services as a tool.

Since I am in Colorado, I am going to use an example from The University of Denver. DU's Career Development Office offers a wealth of information to students. Their Career Development and Opportunities handbook is fantastic and you can read it even if you aren't a student at DU.

Wherever you are attending law school, you need to make sure that you know what services are offered by Career Services. This means going over their website if they have one. It means going in and talking with the people who work at Career Services – on a regular basis. It means sitting down and telling them what you want to do when you graduate. It means using the tools they offer.

Remember, in all likelihood, the people in Career Services know many lawyers in the community. This means that they are a route to you getting to know lawyers in the legal community.

But what if you are going to school in an area you don't want to live and work? This is where your Career Service office may have less tools for you. Be open with them that you are wanting to work outside of the area you are going to school. See who they know who works in the area you want to live. Are there alumni who work in that area? Do they know people in Career Service offices at a school in that area? I've had Career Service people from law schools outside of Colorado contact me to see if I would talk with students who want to move to Colorado and my only connection with the Career Service person is via LinkedIn. So ask for help!

As an aside, take a look at other law schools Career Services websites. Some are good, some are bad. But you will be surprised at some of the very good information you find. For instance, I once found a list of all public interest law firms in the DC area that were offering internships on a law school's Career Service site. So be curious.

C. What Things Do You Like to Do?

The law is vast. Practice areas are not as vast. The journey to figure out a practice area you think you can enjoy seems daunting. But you already know what you like to do outside of the law so use what you like outside of the law as a template to help you determine a practice area.

Are you gregarious? Do you like public speaking? Are you interested in solving problems where two sides disagree and are fighting? Then litigation, broadly speaking, is something you should consider.

Are you business oriented? Do you enjoy planning and

creating? Did you go to school and pursue a business degree? You should consider the transactional and advising side of the law.

For most, this is the big divide: Do you want to do courtroom work or do you want to stay out of court? Of course, just because you want to be in court doesn't mean you will always be trying cases. But litigation and trial work and the lawyers who do this type of work usually aren't drafting contracts or doing business deals and drafting documents. So for most of us, there is a decision to make concerning the court or non-court route.

If you want to go to court, you have another decision. Do you want to practice civil or criminal law? And if you want to practice criminal law, do you want to be a DA or a defense attorney?

Ask yourself these questions. Be truthful to yourself. If you really hate conflict and you really hate public speaking, forcing yourself into litigation is not wise. Conversely, if you don't like drafting documents or reviewing contracts, you probably aren't going to like being a transactional attorney.

Some people will definitely know the area they want to practice. Others have a vague idea. The goal is to narrow down your desired area as fine as possible. This will help you as you begin to network and search for internships and later jobs.

D. Practice Series Books

If you go to your state Bar association you will likely find that they produce practice series books. Unlike law school textbooks, these books tell you and show you how to do things. They are like user manuals for different practice areas. I wish I had known about these books prior to graduating law school.

First, these books are a great overview of what various areas of practice do. If you are interested in Family Law, for instance, the Colorado Bar Association produces a fantastic book on Family Law that covers almost all the major areas of the practice. And you will find that the chapters of these books are written, primarily, by practicing lawyers.

Another nice aspect to these books is that they cover areas of the law that you don't often hear about in law school.

E. Continuing Legal Education Seminars

Attorneys have to take continuing legal education classes to maintain their license to practice. If you want to learn more about a practice area, these are an untapped resource. Many are now online. Although I would suggest going in person if possible so you can network.

CLE's offer you a chance to see what issues practicing attorneys are dealing with. They are much different than a law school class.

In my 20 plus years of practice, I have seen exactly one law student at a CLE.

F. My Story

I knew I wanted to be a litigator. I wasn't sure if I wanted to work on the criminal side or the civil. I was fortunate to have a long clerkship with a civil firm that did a variety of civil litigation. I didn't mind it but I wanted to be in court more. That is what drove me over to the criminal side of the Bar. After doing a clerkship with the Missouri State Public Defenders, I knew that I wanted to practice criminal law.

G. What do You Want?

Ask yourself hard questions about what you want out of your career. It's your career. The right answer for you may be very different than your friend's answer. The right answer for you might be in a non-traditional law job. But, and this is the crucial part, the sooner you narrow down your options, the sooner you can develop an actionable item list for your networking plan.

3) Networking

Once you have decided where you want to live and work and the area of practice you are interested in, you can focus on building a networking plan.

Lawyers and law students tend to lean towards perfectionism. Don't worry about your networking plan being "perfect," rather focus on getting one in place and then executing the plan you have developed.

Your plan will be unique to you. And that is because you are unique. So the steps I suggest don't have to be followed in whole, and you should throw out any you don't like. Heck, maybe you will find all of my suggestions worthless – except for starting to network. And that's fine. My true goal is to help you find what you want from law school.

At the end of this book, you will find an outline and then a one-page sheet. The purpose of these items is to allow you to write down your plan. Again, you don't have to use them. But I encourage you to write your plan down. There is much evidence that we are more likely to accomplish tasks we write down.

A. You're Part of a Profession

Law school doesn't do a good job of welcoming you to the profession. The moment you were accepted to law school you became a part of the legal profession. Every modern lawyer goes to law school. The vast majority take the Bar exam. All recall being in law school and wondering how they were going to find a job. This is a long way of saying that many, many people in the profession are waiting and willing to help you.

B. Get Used to Asking for Help

There is no shame in asking in help. Part of effective networking is asking people to help you. Asking for help is different from asking for a job. And that is one of the nuances of effective networking – you are learning about practice areas and getting to know people but you aren't asking for a job. The jobs and opportunities will come. But they come from relationships and shared interests and having people know who you are and what you can do.

C. Some People Will Say "No"

Some people who you try to network with will say no. It happens. Resolve now to not allow this to stop you. It's part of life. It's not a reflection on you.

If I were writing your networking plan, I would put the word 'resilient' somewhere on the top of the plan. Resilience and consistency are a key trait to any networking plan.

Be resilient.

Be consistent.

Be determined.

If you embrace these three traits, you will overcome the doors that do not open.

D. Get a Plan – Any Plan is Better Than No Plan

Chances are you are a perfectionist. It is a personality trait common in law students. And law school makes this trait even worse. But getting a networking plan written is much more important that making the "perfect" networking plan. You'll never have the perfect plan. Every plan you make will get adjusted and tweaked and revised and maybe even thrown away for a new plan. The key is to get a plan and to start executing on your plan.

Actionable Items: these are the things you can set out to do each day or week. For instance, if you want to move to a new town, you might have as an Actionable Item contacting at least one person on LinkedIn who lives in that town.

Set aside some time every day to make your plan come to life. It doesn't have to be much. 15 minutes a day will add up if you are consistent.

Set reasonable expectations – you won't achieve all your goals immediately.

E. Find a Mentor

Get a mentor! Mentors will help you put your networking plan into action. Mentors often will also give you access to their network. And mentors have a much, much broader view of the legal world than you do as a law student.

How do you find a mentor? Often, your Career Service Office has a list of possible mentors. So do local and state bar associations. But you can also ask a lawyer you know or admire. There are some groups online that can link you to mentors. And there is LinkedIn, which has a large number of people in the legal space who are actively teaching.

Mentors are especially crucial for those of you who are first generation law students. As a first-generation law student, I know the difficulty of not having a ready-made network a parent built. Mentors are a HUGE asset. The sooner you get one, the sooner you are making strides to attack networking from multiple angles.

Final Thoughts

As we leave this chapter, remember: Your networking plan will not be perfect, no matter how much time you devote to planning it. It is far more important to get started and to incorporate actionable items than anything else. And the longer you wait, the harder it gets.

4) Small Markets

Much has changed since I graduated law school in 1998. First among those changes is the rapid growth and acceptance of technology. A person in a small firm has the same access to legal research and case law as a person in a large firm. This didn't used to be the case.

As you start to search for jobs and internships, don't ignore smaller markets. This is especially true if law school hasn't really been your thing and your grades do not reflect your capabilities.

Smaller legal markets are often overlooked. But the law is the same in Grand Junction, Colorado as it is in Denver.

Small legal markets have some definite pluses:

1. Usually a lower cost of living.
2. A smaller Bar so more collegiality.
3. Less competition for jobs.
4. Often you get to handle your own cases faster.
5. The potential to move up the ladder in a firm faster.
6. Greater community.
7. Better commute, if any.
8. The chance to be a part of the legal community and be known.

Smaller markets tend to also have less billable requirements and since the pace of life is, often, less hectic, you get to enjoy your work without having your work become your entire life.

The commute aspect of smaller markets is very nice. It isn't uncommon to have a 5 or 10 minute commute in a smaller market.

I wish I had been encouraged more to pursue a smaller market when I was in law school. As a person who wants to do things rather than contemplate them, I would have loved the opportunity to handle my own cases early in my career and then to advance quicker than is possible in a bigger market.

For those of you who really are looking for community, a smaller market is someplace you should take a serious look at. It's no secret that in many large cities, the sense of community is lacking. And despite the trend for remote work, the reality of the practice of law, especially for younger lawyers is that you spend much of your time working at the office. So community, commute, the things that you are working for, become much more important since you are going to an office most days.

Smaller markets do come with a caveat: not all small markets have every type of legal practice. So if you are wanting to practice federal criminal defense, for instance, living in Eagle, Colorado is not a great place. But Brunswick, Georgia is a small town with a federal courthouse. So do your research, investigate your options.

As more and more people have concentrated into larger metros, there is also the issue of smaller markets having an aging lawyer population. This presents an opportunity for a younger, ambitious lawyer to gain a footing and become a valuable member of a firm in short order.

Don't forget about government jobs in smaller communities. Every town or city will have a city attorney (sometimes a private law firm), the county will have a county attorney's office, there will be a prosecutor's office for the county or district, and there will be some type of public defender. These types of jobs often allow a young lawyer to take on more serious matters much earlier than if they were working in a like-kind larger metro office. And for those who work for a state public defender, even though you are in a small office, you are connected to the much larger system, with its training and resources.

5) The Hidden Job Market and Your 5 Year Plan

Most legal jobs are hidden. At least they are hidden to you as a law student. Why is that? Most firms aren't large enough to have a hiring director. Many government firms have their own ways of finding prospective hires. And many very good firms are only looking to hire people they know – they aren't going to troll through a ton of resumes.

Because so much of the legal market is hidden, the need to get out and find out about the practice is all the more pressing. For some of you, this is an adventure and you enjoy the exploration. For others, this is a nightmare. How are you going to get the doors to open? How can you ask people for help? Where do I start?

No matter if you enjoy the search or not, you need to do it. Unless your strategy is to rely on OCI's. And for some people, OCI's will get the job done. This little book isn't really designed for the OCI crowd, although the suggestions I have will help them build business and gain skills.

Back to the hidden job market, when I left government practice, I had two jobs with law firms before I started my own practice. Neither job was posted. I obtained both through relationships. And my story isn't unique.

There is another aspect of the practice which doesn't get discussed in law school – many of your smaller firms make good money and have a nice work/life balance. It's rare to see a small firm call themselves a "Lifestyle Firm." No doubt there are some that exist, but they are rare.

You discover the hidden job market through your network. And this is an added benefit to networking, you start to see the legal job market that you couldn't see from the confines of law school.

Another good way to discover the hidden job market is to see who is presenting various CLE's. Usually, the people who are presenting at CLE's are interested in networking and their interaction in the CLE world means that they are exposed to a wide variety of legal groups, firms, and people.

Bar Associations are another way to gain exposure to the hidden job market. Check out your state Bar Association. See if there are specialty Bar groups. Specialty Bar groups have many activities and are a wonderful way to gain traction in the world of practicing lawyers.

If I could go back, I would tell my much younger self to view the exploration of the hidden legal market as a bit of a game. Be open to the discovery. Enjoy the process. Have fun. I suspect my younger self might have ignored this advice. That would have been a mistake, one of many.

5 years

Where do you want to be in 5 years? And why 5 years?

Let's take the last question first. At about the 5-year mark of practice, you see the world of the law much differently than when you are at the 1 or 2 year mark. By now, you have been practicing for a sufficient amount of time to understand your practice area, to know many people in the legal community, and you are well on your way to becoming a subject matter expert.

So where do you want to be in 5 years? And how are you going to get there? The answer is yours and only yours as to where you wish to be. But having this goal in mind is helpful. For instance, if you want to be working in-house for a company, it makes little sense to start your legal career as a Public Defender.

The other reason to have a 5-year goal is that it allows you to focus on gaining meaningful experience and skills that allow you to achieve the goal you have set. This goal also gets you focused on you – don't expect that everyplace you work for will have this goal. Some places don't care about your development. This is your career and your professional life; you must take charge.

Sometimes I am asked by students or young lawyers, "What happens if my 5-year goal changes?" It's a good question. Your 5-year goal isn't set in stone. That is not the purpose. The purpose is to give you a metric by which to keep moving forward. You want to be moving forward at this point in your legal career, expanding your options, maximizing your potential, and achieving the goals that you set out. And, likely, your 5-year goal will change, at least a bit.

Lawyers who set goals achieve them. Lawyers who wait for others to discover how spectacular they are find themselves disappointed.

As we move to the next chapter, keep this at the forefront of your mind: Nobody else will champion you the way you champion yourself. This isn't being selfish. It isn't being arrogant. It's the reality of life and the practice of law.

Some of you may need some coaching in order to feel comfortable being your own champion. That's ok. If this is you, reach out. I'd love to be your coach and if I am not a good fit, I can give you some referrals to those who might be a good fit. I strongly encourage you to get some coaching if you are an agreeable person as being your own champion is much harder for you than for those of us who are not as agreeable.

If you are interested in working with me as your coach, my information is at the end of this book.

6) Adjuncts

During my time in law school, I took several classes taught by adjuncts. These lawyers were active in the profession. They had hundreds of contacts. They were doing what I wanted to do. Exactly what I wanted to do. So what did I do? I went to class and never once asked my adjuncts for help. Not once. This, looking back, was one of the biggest mistakes I ever made in law school. Stupid doesn't begin to cover my failure to act.

But you have an advantage. You can learn from my failure.

Your adjuncts are a hidden source, a hidden wealth of information and contacts. They are practicing attorneys. They are good at it too, otherwise they wouldn't be teaching as adjuncts. These attorneys are there, at your law school, because they want to teach. They want to help. And that means that there is a 99.9% chance that if you ask them to assist you in networking, they will help you.

Nobody ever told me I should seek out my adjuncts for networking help.

I never thought of asking them for help. I should have. I should have asked every single one for help. I should have asked them the questions I needed answered, like:

1. How did you get started?

2. Do you know of any internships?
3. What can I do to become the type of lawyer that you are?
4. Do you know other lawyers that I can connect with and talk to?
5. What classes should I take that would be helpful?
6. What questions should I be asking?
7. What can I do to be more competitive in getting a job in this type of law?

I do recall some people in my classes taught by adjuncts taking time to talk to them. Some of my classmates were way ahead of me in taking advantage of the opportunities that law school provided. That said, none of my classmates viewed the adjuncts as a networking source.

As I look back, I threw away opportunities to network with at least 10 lawyers who were practicing law in the area that I wanted to practice. Some of those lawyers would later go on to become judges. All remain well respected. All had and have deep connections to the legal community.

In terms of a layup, this suggestion is it. Every single law school has adjuncts.

Don't ask for a job! That is not how to approach your adjuncts. Rather, approach your adjuncts as a bridge between academia and the practice of law.

As an example, if I were an adjunct professor teaching criminal defense topics and I had a student approach me who wanted to become a criminal defense lawyer or a prosecutor, I could give that student plenty of valuable, actionable information in about 30 minutes. Any other adjunct could do the same for their area of practice.

I am often asked how to start networking with practicing attorneys. This suggestion is a very easy way to get started.

7) LinkedIn

How I wish that LinkedIn existed when I was in law school. As a first generation lawyer, I could have learned so much. If you are not on LinkedIn as a law student, that needs to change.

Get a profile. Make sure your profile has a good headshot. Let people know you are in law school.

Connect with lawyers who are practicing law. Engage with the lawyers who post. Once you have engaged, then send a DM. You're much more likely to get a response as opposed to an unannounced DM right when you connect.

LinkedIn is both a learning tool and a networking tool.

As a learning tool, LinkedIn gets you connected to some of the real thought leaders in the law student space, like Jordan Gardner and Amanda Haverstick both of whom are working to make law school easier for you. And you also get a chance to experience the work of people like Ross Guberman – he WILL make you a better legal writer.

As a networking tool, LinkedIn allows you to see and interact with lawyers practicing the type of law you want to practice. And everyone on LinkedIn is on it to interact. So once you start engaging, it's normal to DM other people and establish more in depth relationships.

LinkedIn is also a space where you can make posts saying what you want to do. If you tell people that you are a law student and your goal is to practice insurance defense, you will get responses and likely will get contacted with advice.

I firmly believe that most law students don't utilize LinkedIn to their advantage. But that doesn't have to be your experience. You can use it to your advantage and if you do, it's a platform that offers you much for free.

My advice to any law student is to devote 15 minutes a day to LinkedIn. Add connections. Interact and comment on relevant posts. Start posting yourself. Do this every single day for 90 days and you will be surprised at all the information and contacts you will have gained. All for free.

LinkedIn is invaluable if you plan on moving to a city where you didn't go to law school or grow up. I have helped several people find law jobs in Colorado via our LinkedIn connections.

So how do you best use LinkedIn? Connect. Engage. Post. DM. Do this and you will have new friends and colleagues. And this network will continue to grow and will follow you after law school.

There is another reason to be on LinkedIn – you learn about marketing and sales. I cannot recommend enough following and connecting with Cooper Saunders. Cooper isn't a lawyer, but he will revolutionize how you view opportunity if you read his books and follow him.

8) Why You Need to Start Following the Legal Job Market

Do you follow the legal job market? I didn't when I was in law school. I should have.

It's much easier today. But why should you? I wrote about the hidden legal job market earlier. Along with the legal job market being largely hidden, many legal jobs you have never heard about because your law school isn't talking about them.

How do you follow the legal job market? Here's what I do:

1. Indeed: go to the geographic area you have interest and search under "lawyer" or "attorney." Do this on a weekly basis and see what jobs are posted. See what they want in terms of experience. This is a great way to find out what you need to do to get those jobs.
2. Go to your state bar's website. Go to their job site. Review all of the jobs.
3. Go to groups like the National Legal Aid and Defenders website and look at their job postings.
4. Take a look at the Association of Corporate Counsel website and look at their career postings.
5. USA Jobs – the federal government job site. Search "attorney."
6. State job websites – search "attorney."

7. Fd.org – lists almost all federal public defender jobs.
8. DOJ's website – AUSA job postings and other DOJ attorney jobs.
9. NeoGov – lists a ton of government jobs.
10. City and County websites – often list attorney jobs.
11. Find your states' Prosecutor Association – search their job postings.

Since you are in law school, many of these jobs are not likely entry level. That isn't the point. The point is to educate yourself about the type of legal jobs that exist.

Do this and you might find a niche you are interested in pursuing. Some of these jobs you will never hear about if you aren't doing what I suggest in this chapter.

9) Closing Thoughts

This book contains the advice I would give myself if I were starting law school all over. It's the advice I will give my son should he decide to go to law school. It's the advice I wish I had before I went to law school.

No doubt you will not agree with everything I suggest. That's fine, modify any of the advice so that it fits your plan.

If you take only one piece of advice I offer, I hope it is this: Start networking now.

The advice works. I have seen law students who follow the advice this book offers get internship and jobs. I have seen law students who follow this advice successfully move from a state they are attending law school to a new state where they have no contacts. And I believe so much in the advice offered in this book that I wrote it.

I appreciate you for trusting me by purchasing this book. I'm rooting for you and if I can help, please reach out.

If you want more help than this book provided, I would love to work with you. We all need a coach. If you think that we'd be a good fit, I look forward to helping you achieve your career goals. If you want to get some coaching, please call my office at 720-613-8783 or email me at millermleonard@gmail.com and put "Coaching" in the subject line.

10) Appendix 1

Quick Outline

1. **Where do you want to live?**
    a) Just because you are going to law school in a city of state, doesn't mean that is where you want to practice.
    b) Knowing where you want to live and practice will help you target your networking plan.
    c) Figure out where you want to live and work.
    d) Smaller markets are overlooked.

2. **What type of law do you think you want to practice?**
    a) Trial work and litigation?
    b) Transactional work?
    c) Non-traditional legal routes?

3. **How to learn about practice areas?**
    a) Take a class in that area.
    b) Go to the state or local bar association and go through practice sets – these books are all about a specific practice area. They are very good.
    c) Look at on-going CLE's offered to practicing lawyers. Go to these and learn about the practice areas – and meet people in those areas.

- d) Talk to adjunct faculty who are practicing in the area you have interest.
- e) Use LinkedIn to establish connections with practicing lawyers in the areas you have interest.
- f) Go to court. It's free. There are many different practice areas at work in the court.

4. **Once you have identified practice areas, now what?**
   - a) Contact lawyers doing what you want to do. Ask to meet, grab coffee, or have a phone call.
   - b) Have questions ready if you can meet or connect.
   - c) Don't expect a job – look to make further connections.
   - d) Try to understand what hiring managers in an area of practice are looking for? For instance, do you need to do a clinic in that area? Are there certain internships that are helpful?
   - e) Try to figure out how a person gets started in the practice area, how to progress, and what it looks like 5 – 10 years down the road.

5. **Design your networking plan for consistency**
   - a) It's not a sprint, it's a marathon.
   - b) Schedule daily time to work on your plan.
   - c) Set up check points – every two or three months, go over your progress.

6. **Be bold but not rude**
   - a) You are selling yourself – so get used to contacting people you don't know.
   - b) On LinkedIn, connect and comment on posts before

sending DM messages.

c) Ask people you meet or talk to if they can introduce you to people.

7. Follow up

a) The sooner you learn that there is no set route to a job, the better off you are.

b) Follow up on suggestions, contacts, and tips.

c) If you have been given help, follow up with a thank you letter or email.

8. Don't lose hope

a) This isn't a short-term plan.

b) Don't expect to get a job or an internship right away.

c) Like running a distance race, don't focus on the end as much as you focus on taking the next step.

d) If you take the daily steps, you will soon find that you have a large network.

9. Don't overlook OCI's

a) Do as many OCI's as possible.

b) You might find that your networking helps you in your OCI's.

10. Be open and inquisitive

a) The more you learn about the practice, the more you can tailor your networking.

b) Much of law is sales. Developing your network helps you become a person who gets business.

c) The practice area you end up wanting to pursue might not be what you originally thought.

11) Appendix 2

Questions to Ask Yourself
Practice Questions:
1. What is your 5 year goal:
2. Are you interested in working for the government:
3. Litigation/trial or transactional:
4. Civil or criminal trial work:
5. Where do you want to live (rank them):

Questions about you:
1. Where is your family located:
2. Do you want to be located away from family:
3. How important is it to fit in with the "values" of the area you live in:
4. Do you describe yourself as conservative, liberal, or does it matter:
5. Are there types of law you know you have zero interest in practicing:
6. Are you interested in a clerkship:

www.ingramcontent.com/pod-product-compliance
Lightning Source LLC
Chambersburg PA
CBHW050320220526
45465CB00005B/2067